Wakefield Press

Flying with Cranes

Born and raised in Adelaide, Heather Caddick has had a diverse career spanning kindergarten teaching to stockbroking and investment. She is passionate about voluntary work encompassing wildlife and humanitarian causes. When not travelling she lives in Adelaide with her husband Alfie.

This is her fourth book.

By the same author

For the Love of Rhinos

The Road Less Travelled

This Life in Rhymes and Riddles

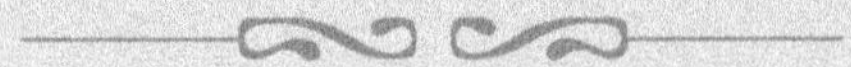

Flying with Cranes
(and other stories)

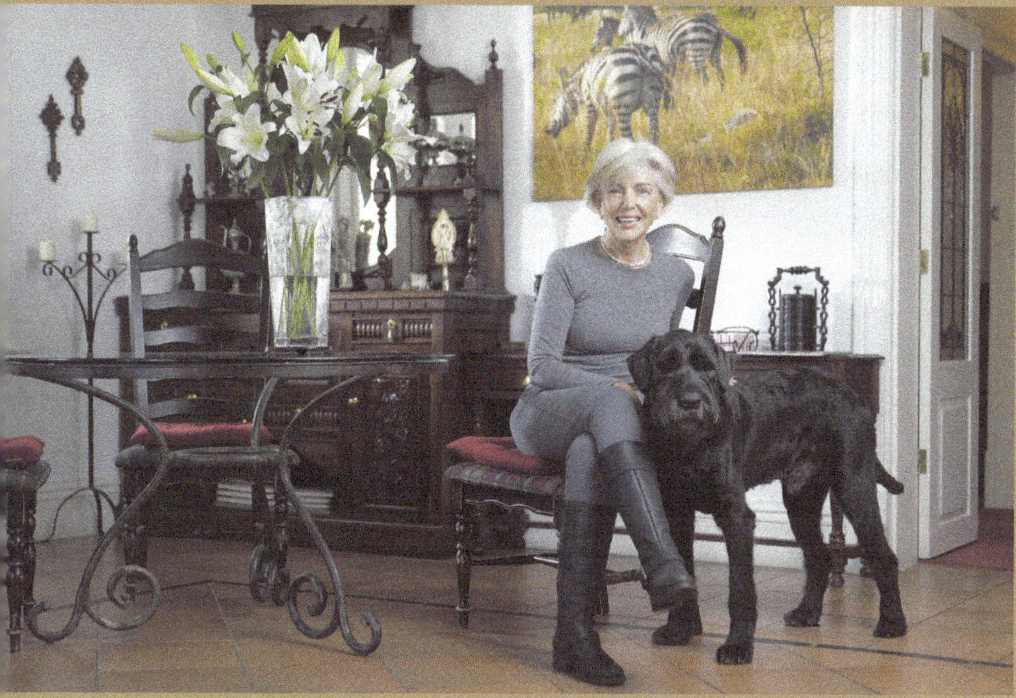

Heather Caddick

Wakefield Press
16 Rose Street
Mile End
South Australia 5031
www.wakefieldpress.com.au

First published 2021

Edited by Julia Beaven, Wakefield Press
Designed by Liz Nicholson, Wakefield Press
Typeset by Michael Deves, Wakefield Press

ISBN 978 1 74305 809 1

A catalogue record for this book is available from the National Library of Australia

For Tilda, Emmy, Natalia and Annabel

Contents

Author's Note

This book continues to showcase snapshots of the human condition, with adventures in Romania, Czech Republic and Iran, Africa and the Ukraine, as well as stories of the natural world of wildlife and wild habitats.

If we can work towards a balance between human life and wildlife, we can guarantee there will be a better world for our children and grandchildren.

Flying with Cranes

Depend on it, that the lovers of freedom will be free.

EDMUND BURKE

It is March, and there is the promise of spring in Sweden. Lake Hornborga, north of Gothenburg, is a sea of cranes, thousands of cranes that have flown here from Spain, congregating on the banks to rest and refuel. Courting pairs dance and leap as they reaffirm their lifelong bonds with bugle blasts and raucous shrieks. Mesmerising to watch, they bob and bow and pirouette with ruffled feathers.

They'll spend five weeks here before moving to the far north of Sweden to breed. They tower at 1.3 metres, with elongated necks, black and white head stripes, grey plumage and a bustle of feathers at the rear.

Courtship begins. A male follows a female in a stately march-like walk. The female calls out in a high note, and the male responds with a scream. Copulation is similarly dramatic.

For Swedes, this annual migration is of huge folkloric significance, heralding the onset of spring. Once the cranes feasted on tubers left over from the harvest for Swedish vodka, but today 150 tonnes of grain is deposited on Lake Hornborga's banks to supplement the craned diet. Festive events are staged to coincide with the annual migration. Volunteers keep count; 19,500 cranes the highest number registered so far.

In May they depart for the final leg of their journey. In the far

north of Sweden they find small and swampy clearings among the pine forests. It is quiet and peaceful here away from human activity. They paint their bodies with mud from the swamp in order to blend with the nesting environment and for 30 days or so the parents share the task of sitting on the two eggs in a nest 90 centimetres in diameter.

New hatchlings can swim soon after hatching and when 24 hours old can run with their parents. By nine weeks they fly short distances, and during this time the adults go through their post-breeding moult, leaving them flightless for five or six weeks and vulnerable to predators such as eagles or domestic dogs. When under attack, the cranes jab with their bills, or hit out with their wings and kick with their feet. This aggression is usually successful, protecting them and their chicks from predators.

Cranes can benefit farmers by consuming waste grain from harvested fields. They eat roots, rhizomes, tubers, leaves, fruits, seeds and berries – the cranberry is named after them. The mothers will regurgitate their food to give to their young.

When ready to return to Spain, they can be seen flying together in flocks of up to 400 birds, a thousand metres above the earth, the height of their migration only bettered by the Ruppell's griffon vulture and the bar-headed goose. They will stage sites en route, where they rest and feed, and so the cycle continues, to be repeated again the following year.

Iran - Smooth As Silk

How easy it is when destiny proves kind,
with full-spread sails to run before the wind

JOHN DRYDEN

It's a relief to leave shaking heads and doom prophets behind, as I fly to Shiraz to spend three weeks exploring Iran. With swathed scarf and arms covered, I still stand out as a nonlocal. A young Iranian approaches. He gives me his contact details saying, 'If you need help please contact me, I want you to enjoy our beautiful country.'

It's a mere 20-minute progression through security in Shiraz by polite and respectful officials. The 5 am streets of Shiraz are deserted as Reza, my taxi driver, speeds to the Home Hotel. A pink glow over stark mountains bordering this fertile valley promises a beautiful sunrise, and reveals boulevards canopied by trees and gardens.

Reza says, 'The French and Australians took our name to brand their wine, and it's now illegal for us to drink.' Then, with a wink, 'But we all do!'

I book Reza to take me to a mountaintop to watch the sunset, and settle in the hotel, spending time over my breakfast of fresh olives and feta with warm pita bread and samovar-brewed tea.

The hotel's traditional Persian garden with pools and waterways is a perfect place to ease time-zone changes, and the enormous marble foyer a great place to people watch. Beautiful Iranian

Heather and Alfie in Shiraz.

Heather with friends at Persepolis, Iran.

women, their scarves well back from their foreheads, wearing flowing silk tops over Capri pants and designer sunglasses, gather for tea, laughing as the latest gossip is exchanged.

Nearby in leather chairs a group of elders are in serious discussion. A grand piano is being played by a talented pianist as an elegant woman with attaché case enters the foyer and proceeds to direct three men, confidently conducting a meeting in one of the alcoves.

It is now early evening and with Reza at the wheel we set off to see the sunset, but I'm soon clutching my seatbelt as he combats heavy traffic by weaving past trucks and buses at a ferocious speed. I remind him the sun is about to drop in five minutes, where is the mountaintop? He pulls over to park and hauls me up a cliff face, thick with thorn bushes, to a small ridge where we sit to watch the blood-red sun drop behind the mountain range. The homeward drive is less frenetic, and I'm happy to return to the serenity of the Persian garden.

My bloke arrives the following morning. We walk to the Pink Mosque, an astounding building with intricate mosaic tiling and an enormous dome surrounding a courtyard pool. We are approached constantly by Iranians wanting to befriend us, curious as to where we live. They comment, 'I send peace to your country,' and, 'Please tell people to come and visit us.' They offer us lunch in their private homes.

A schoolteacher asks if we would speak English with his pupils and we do so, only to find these 10-year-olds are already fluent.

We intend to hire local drivers and steer away from tour groups that often filter experiences through a rigid agenda. Our plan is to drive to Yazd and Isfahan, then to the oasis city of Kashan.

The desert city of Yazd was an ancient commerce centre for silk carpets and textiles. Mud-brick Qajar-era houses have wind towers for thermal cooling, and there is a labyrinth of lanes and bazaars. Wandering along a laneway we are invited for tea by the proprietor of a small hotel with a garden courtyard. We sip tea to birdsong and tinkling water from a fountain shrouded by pomegranate trees.

'Sanctions are biting, but we are resilient and just get on with our lives,' the proprietor says. He suggests we drive to Koupane, where there is a restored caravanserai to stay overnight.

Mohammed is our new driver, and mercifully his car has air conditioning, but he seems to be lost, and studies his phone constantly as we weave through traffic. He does not speak English, and my Farsi is limited to '*salaam*'. I discover that he speaks German, so my bloke barks directions from our Lonely Planet book, I translate to German for Mohammed, who relays directions to a colleague in Farsi as a vividly decorated truck passes us with a camel peeping its head over the back tray. We finally arrive in Koupane.

Silk Road caravanserai were built every 40 kilometres across Iran, measuring one day's camel train journey, and providing a place to rest and to trade. The Koupane caravanserai has been exquisitely restored and surrounds a garden courtyard. Its lofty alcoves have been converted to luxury accommodation, with Persian carpets and comfy divans on the ground floor, and a sleeping chamber at the top of a spiral staircase. Mosaic-glass windows filter light and the Persian garden is at our front door.

Our next destination is Isfahan, where the world's largest town square is bordered by an extraordinary bazaar and two

Gardeners at work in Shiraz.

Heather and Alfie in Kashan, Iran, 2019.

A morning chess game in Shiraz, 2019.

mosques. We walk to the square, attracted by the beating of drums and tooting of trumpets, just in time to see a polo match.

Persia invented polo centuries ago, and this enormous square has staged polo games since 1600 AD. Isfahan locals are out in force to support their teams.

The bazaar borders the square with lofty arches and alleyways crammed with carpet sellers, jewellers, spices, antiquities and delectable confectionary. Bazaars are still the prime meeting place for friends and families and for business dealings in Iran. The atmosphere here is infectious with laughter and shouts of delight from children, and a mish mash of Iranian life emerging at the end of a hot summer's day.

I decide to try a Persian bath at the Qazi bathhouse in Isfahan. Built in 1600, it is marble lined and domed, with mosaic skylights.

Two bath ladies are my attendants, buxom and with personalities to match they joke and laugh together as I'm instructed to lie on a marble slab. They scrub every inch of my skin with what feels like sandpaper, then there's a dousing with spa water, a massage of pummelling ending with resounding slaps down my backbone, and immersion into another pool. A sarong is then wrapped around me and I'm led to a room to relax and refresh with iced lemon mint and saffron syrup, feeling reborn.

Our next local driver is Ali for the three-hour drive to Kashan, an ancient desert oasis, now a busy city, with an UNESCO-branded Persian garden.

Spa water streams from underground, filtered into ducts and pools transecting a formal garden of astounding beauty, with canopies of mature trees, flowering shrubs, and garden beds of tangerine and yellow zinnias.

We are befriended by a local Iranian family and invited to lunch at their home. This generous hospitality has been shown every day we've spent in Iran.

We move on to Teheran, and take an overnight train to Tabriz, once part of Azerbaijan. It's a pleasant change to take a train after driving the freeways, and again we are the focus of kindness and curiosity from train passengers.

Tabriz boasts the world's largest bazaar at seven-square kilometres and more treasures to discover on our last days in Iran.

With every warning and preconceived notion now upturned, we have Iran at the top of our list for a return visit.

Romania and the Danube Delta

Some good advice from one who knows,
take twice the cash and half the clothes

ANON

It is May 2019 and we are in Bucharest heading for the old town, driving along tree-lined boulevards bordered by gardens. Hotel Volo overlooks the river, beyond the former President Ceausescu's Palace.

Smiling young girls promenade the boulevards window shopping among collections of people walking on the pavements, taking coffee and socialising. The atmosphere is friendly and inclusive. Mahar ('Call me Mike') greets us and shows us to our room, as the door handle falls off. 'No problems, we'll fix it,' says Mike, and wanders away.

We decide to walk to the Palace, surrounded by beautiful parks and gardens. A *babushka* is sweeping paths, joggers run by linked to podcasts, young families with children are playing on swings, and the sun shines in a clear sky.

The Ceausescu Palace is now Parliament House, but the lower floor is an art gallery, and the public are welcome. The days of Ceaucescu's regime are a past horror, buried by the Government, but never forgotten. The extent of Ceaucescu's power is exemplified by an underground maze of roads and offices directly under the Palace, a construction larger than the

Pentagon. During Ceausescu's rule, the KGB and all Eastern Bloc countries had their offices here. A taxi driver tells me it can take half an hour to drive through this underground consortium.

We wander back through the gardens and note an absence of vagrants or beggars, presumably they have moved to wealthier countries. The young are working, positive and upwardly mobile, and there is a real feeling of a country recovering from the oppression of the past; catching up with the rest of the world.

The old town has cobbled streets and a magnificent Orthodox monastery. There are little coffee shops spilling out onto the pavements, fruit and vegetable shops, bakeries and restaurants. We finally return to the Volo Hotel, where Mike offers us lunch and we sit under shady trees adjacent to the hotel eating salads and drinking the local beer.

I am off to the ballet at the Opera House. *Gizelle* is to be performed, and my $15 ticket buys a box in the dress circle. The ushers are ballet students, all dressed in long red gowns with their hair tied back, and their elegance and grace promising a wonderful show to come.

The mezzanine floor is curtained, with high standing tables where champagne and aperitifs are on offer. Soon it is time to assemble in the theatre, where every seat is booked, and everyone is dressed up. Young girls in ballet dresses have their hair tied back with satin ribbons. The performance is outstanding and reflects the importance of the arts and culture during oppressive times. I marvel at the way Romania has nurtured ballet throughout this period.

We are taking a train to Constanta in south-eastern Romania and board an ancient carriage filling with people to make the

Downtown Bucharest.

Dracula's birthplace, Sighisoara, Romania.

three-hour journey. We traverse lush green fields of agriculture, largely owned by foreign nationals for export to their own countries. Romania misses out.

Passengers exchange fruit and biscuits, and there is a delightful communal atmosphere. We are offered pears and biscuits and join in the fun of sharing, despite the lack of language.

Constanta is perched on a hill overlooking the Black Sea and we decide to stay at the Hotel Carol, an older style with Italianate decor and a very prim madame in charge. She conducts us to a room of gentle elegance with french windows overlooking the sea.

We decide to explore, wandering down the steep winding path to the seashore where a fish restaurant is set up on the sand. We enjoy the most amazing array of seafood, fried to a frazzle, with chips piled to the side.

The maitre' d speaks perfect English and we hear about the crowds in high season. Thankfully we have dodged them and are almost alone. It is surreal to look out over the tidal expanse of sand and water, and consider all the different countries that share these Black Sea shores.

We are heading to the Danube Delta. The uncle of the receptionist at the Carol Hotel offers to take us, thrilled to receive hard currency, so we race along deserted roads in his BMW at 150 kph. He reassures us, 'We all drive like this in Romania.' We arrive at Tulcea, bid our driver farewell and board a water taxi for Sulima, the gateway to the Delta.

We have chosen to stay at Casa Coral. A huge dining room is being set up for a local school formal, tables are decorated in flamboyant colours and red balloons are tied to every chair.

'Lady in Red' is being played as the students assemble, dressed to the nines, chatting and laughing. We realise there won't be much sleep tonight, and pre-dinner drinks on the verandah overlooking the river is a pleasant diversion.

The river is lined with water taxis and boats for hire next day. We choose Dave and his boat for our cruise along the vast Danube Delta, its lakes, streams and waterways bordered by bulrushes and greenery. Waterlilies bloom in glades, and pelicans, cormorants and egrets soar above, occasionally swooping to retrieve fish from the pristine waters.

We are grateful to Dave for charting our course, marvelling at how far the delta extends. There is no sound when we cut the motor and drift into a backwater to sit and watch birds, butterflies and bees going about their business in this extraordinary haven of nature.

Our next adventure is to investigate Transylvania and the historic town of Sighisoara, whose history goes back to Roman times. During the 16th century Sighisoara became a centre of excellence in the trades. The wealth created by craftsmen allowed the town to build a strong defence system of towers, with bastions for armaments. Each tower was built and maintained by a trade guild. The enormous citadel was built by the Saxons in the 12th century, and only goldsmiths, tailors, carpenters and tinsmiths were allowed to have their guilds inside the citadel.

Exploring is a challenge among Sighisoara's winding cobbled streets, stairways and tiny square, but we finally reach the citadel, where horse-drawn carts ferry the tourists around. There are markets, coffee shops and ice cream stalls, and dominating the scene is a huge clock tower emitting commanding bongs as the

Timber being transported through the Carpathian Mountains.

Top: Romanian engine drivers pause for a smoko, 2018.
Above: A steam locomotive following the Vaser River, Carpathian Mountains.

time is marked. We hire a horse-drawn cart, and gently travel the lanes and alleyways, lost in a time of days gone by.

Everywhere there are masks and capes for sale, marking the birthplace of Vlad Dracula, who ruled the province in the 15th century, and who inspired the fictional creation of Count Dracula. We finally return to the town and find a tiny restaurant embedded in the hillside, to take lunch overlooking the city.

It's now time to head north to the Carpathian Mountains to experience the Vaser Valley railway, boasting the last remaining working wood-burning steam trains in Europe. The 60 kilometres of track twists and turns over bridges and through tunnels alongside the Vaser River, revealing a vast forest devoid of roads and villages. The purpose of the railway, built in 1932, was to bring timber down the valley to the sawmills.

The tourist steam train operates along these tracks in spring and summer, and we board in Viseu de Sus. The engine is belching smoke and steaming away in preparation for the journey. We climb into an antique carriage, complete with carved wooden window frames and doors, and upholstered seats faded with use. Local families board – grandmas, parents, sisters and brothers and a couple of babies. With a lurch we set off to the *clackety clack* of wheels on the line and the *chuff chuff* of the steam engine.

We are entering virgin forest with no sign of human habitation, and gently wind along the river to our destination. Trees, creepers and bushes bursting with coloured flowers give way to the train. With the carriage windows open, we are able to feel part of it all.

We come to a clearing where the trees are felled and the engine stops to allow us to get off and take coffee and cakes,

seated around tables overlooking the river. Many people speak English and approach us to ask where we're from and to chat before the engine driver, wearing a black singlet exposing a mammoth physique, toots the horn for departure and we board the train for the homeward journey.

We arrive and see a horse-drawn cart galloping along the road, with a pregnant woman lying on a sack in the back blowing gum. The driver is standing and whipping the horse to speed up. The two carts following are driven by kids, dark skinned with black curly hair, filthy, screaming and laughing. They are gypsies, and a law unto themselves. With this indelible image we leave enigmatic, historic and surprising Romania.

B&B sitting room, Sighisoara, Romania, 2018.

The Destruction of Madagascar

It is far easier to act under conditions of tyranny,
than to think

HANNAH ARENDT

I leave Antananarivo (Tana) for a guided tour of Madagascar. My mission is to view lemurs in the wild, and to see for myself the clearing of forests and their conversion to rice paddies.

My driver Bari crawls through the narrow streets before we stop suddenly. There is a roadblock ahead to allow the President's cavalcade to pass, with ten motorcycles followed by two police cars, then a flash black limousine for the President, and a troop of police behind. We are finally free to crawl away, and after some nifty driving along back streets we are in the countryside.

I am unprepared for the unmaintained roads of potholes and grooves. We crawl and bump from ditch to drain in a car with no shock absorbers. I find it hard to adjust to the swings and bounces and feel nauseous.

The soil is black and can grow anything and there are mango trees bougainvillea and flowering shrubs dotting the roadside; small rice paddy holdings are neatly squared. These are passed on from generation to generation and represent subsistence or survival.

We are on the eastern side of Madagascar, which is Asian, and due to the population explosion more forest is being cleared for rice paddies, denuding the country of its natural habitat.

The country is 50/50 Christian Anglican and Catholic, but religion is infiltrated with cultural history, originally from Indonesia. When someone dies, the deceased is wrapped in silk and buried in a family cemetery. Seven years later the body will be dug up to be wrapped again in silk to keep the bones warm. This occasion is celebrated with dignity, followed by a feast and party where all family members will assemble to pay their respects to the dead, seven years after they have died.

We stop at a street market and see wonderful fruit and veg displayed from hessian sacks and cardboard boxes. Scarves draped over wooden poles provide makeshift protection from the weather.

Armed with bananas to quell my car sickness we return to the navigation of such appalling roads that our journey takes seven hours, at an average speed of 10 kph, as we bounce and veer through the maze of potholes.

At last we come to a lake and I bid goodbye to Bari as I board a launch to the Palarium Resort. This is an hour's journey through ancient French-built canals that connect a series of lakes. There are fishermen in dugout canoes quietly fishing and waving us on. The undergrowth is dense both sides of the launch, with birds swooping and calling and fish jumping and spilling back into the water.

On arrival there are endless steps to climb to the bungalows. Luggage is dumped as I am urged to join a group to see lemurs on a nearby island, the last sanctuary for the aye-aye. Only six remain here. They are safe from predators, but have not bred, and will eventually die out. These breeds are now hard to find, as most lemurs are hybrid. They are gentle, inquisitive, playful

creatures and observe us with alert intelligence as we disturb their peace and tranquillity.

It's an hour's journey back by launch and, totally exhausted, I climb the stairs to my bungalow and order a Harpoon gin and tonic and relax on the little balcony overlooking the waterway below.

There is a resident chameleon snoozing on a branch tickling the balustrade, and lemurs are everywhere. They sit on chair backs overlooking your shoulder hoping for fruit. The lemurs have interbred and are accustomed to humans, reliant on being fed and being cared for. This tourist attraction gives a false impression of resilience, whereas the true story of their future existence lies in the wild, a wild that is being drastically cleared and reduced.

At breakfast I share papaya, pineapple and bananas with the lemurs, and then set off by boat through the glorious canal channels to meet with Bari, my driver, and endure another five hours of nausea before finally reaching Antsirabe.

Antsirabe is Madagascar's second city, and a former thermal spa town for the French. I take a *pousse-pousse* to the market where exquisite embroidery is on sale among the fruit and vegetable stores, and I select a wall-hanging of life in Madagascar, embroidered with brightly coloured thread, and depicting everything from village market places to rural scenes of toil and trouble, animals and children playing.

We are heading to Jardin du Roy, and again the roads prove to be a challenge. Groups of young boys cluster around potholes they have filled; they dance in front of our car, making us stop and pay them for the service. This is one way for them to make

money and, as we depart, they dig out the potholes and prepare to repeat the process. This is done with laughter and energy and is tremendous fun for them.

We approach a circle of jagged rocks and in the centre is Jardin du Roy, the best hotel in the country, with horse treks on offer, tennis, a pool and a quiet dignity from the employees.

Villagers are burning the surrounds in protest that their land is not being compensated by National Parks. They must have had prior warning because with a swoop the President's plane lands on the hotel's airstrip. Almost immediately a fleet of cars, sirens blaring, pull up as support.

It's rather like a Bond movie. Scores of black-attired bullyboys accompany the President to the hotel, positioning themselves at strategic points. They are fully armed, wearing Ray-Ban sunglasses and jack boots.

The President is an insignificant-looking little man, who wanders down to the pool where I'm sunbaking, greets me with a '*Bonjour, madame*', and walks on. I would like to mention the state of the roads in Madagascar, but as he spends his time flying, I doubt he would care. He is corrupt and disliked. Ninety-two per cent of Madagascar's population exisits on two dollars a day, and his recent $1 million fireworks party, where his wife wore an $8000 dress, only adds fuel to the fire.

After two days of respite the President takes off in his plane, avoiding the roads, as I arm myself for another nauseous car journey to Tulear. I give out pencils and notebooks to children on the way. There is no schooling and the poverty is tangible, with young children caring for babies and seas of humanity desperately trying to survive.

From Tulear it is a short flight to Tana, where we drive through the former grand enclave of French-built mansions, now government offices. Children are playing soccer in a park nearby. We wind, turn and finally climb a hill to view the Catholic cathedral that perches on a precipice overlooking the city. It feels as though I am in a time warp as I watch the faithful attending church, sealed from the reality of life outside this compound.

I leave Madagascar with a sense of despair at the impossible task of preserving what was once a haven for nature. The balance between human life and wildlife has been irreparably damaged.

The Faroe Islands

The accent of a man's country dwells in his mind and in his heart

FRANCOIS DE LA ROCHEFOUCAULD

The Faroe Islands is a self-governing entity that is part of the Kingdom of Denmark. The archipelago lies between Iceland and Norway and comprises 18 rocky volcanic islands linked together by tunnels, bridges and causeways. Norsemen settled here.

The word 'Faroe' in Old Norse means sheep, and so these are the Sheep Islands, where sheep outnumber humans two to one.

We fly Atlantic Airways to Vagar airport and I'm apprehensive as we approach. I've been told that pilots train on this runway; with its strong cross winds it is considered to be one of the world's most dangerous airports. Mercifully the day is calm, and we approach across a jagged coastline and crashing waves to land, smooth as silk, on the runway.

A small bus ferries us to Torshavn, the capital, a cluster of buildings around a fishing port. The houses are brightly painted, and fish shops and small cafes line the wharves, where fishermen tend to their boats and mend their nets.

Many houses have turf roofs. It rains 300 days a year, and this ancient practice provides protection from the rain. Sheep are used to mow the grass on the roof tops; some even have shrubs and flowers blooming.

Our hotel, perched on a hill, has a turf roof and is completely

modernised and immaculate inside, with minimalist decor and windows overlooking Torshavn and the bay.

The population is around 22,000 people and five bus lines filter out to surrounding islands. All buses are free and provide a regular if rather limited service. We decide to board a bus for the historic city of Kirkjubour. It is a 20-minute journey from Torshavn and the weather is closing in with wind gusts and rain as we gently navigate the road, sheep wandering about and the driver weaving around to dodge them. There are a couple of locals on the bus and we settle in to enjoy the ride.

Kirkjubour's history goes back to the 12th century. It has retained the custom of houses painted black with turf roofs, and with the glum grey weather this scene just accentuates the drama of the place.

The Faroes have no natural forests and wood for the houses was gleaned from driftwood from Norway that beached itself here. The turf roofs were added to protect the houses from rain and wind.

We visit a house built in 1550 AD, now a museum, and home to sheep and an old farmer, who offers us coffee and the chance to buy fresh mutton.

St Olav's Church, built in the 12th century, is still in use and sits in an enclave overlooking the bay. Painted white it marks a contrast with the black buildings below. We walk to the water in blinding wind and rain, and then head back to the bus stop for the return trip to Torshavn.

Our next adventure is a ferry trip to Mykines, a far-west island, free of cars and so remote it has only ten inhabitants. This is a 45-minute ride over rolling waves and I'm extremely

relieved to disembark after we sail through the high rise of basalt columns into a small bay bordered by tall basalt cliffs. A steep staircase leads us past boathouses and green meadows to the tiny village that lies snugly in a green hollow, with a river dissecting it all.

There is a fine collection of turf-roofed houses and a local café, the Mykinesstova, is open for a welcome coffee and cakes. We decide to hike to the lighthouse, promising us a close view of thousands of puffins nesting on the verdant hills along the way.

Puffins are sea birds; they live on the sea and only come to land when it is nesting time. They prepare a burrow over a metre deep, usually on a grassy verge above the cliffs. Baby puffins, or pufflings, hatch and for the first few weeks remain in the burrow, leaving in mid-August to return to the sea.

We are astounded at their numbers; pufflings are staggering around gaining strength by walking and flapping their wings. They are oblivious to our presence, and we gently wander along the winding path, marvelling at this amazing spectacle. Occasionally we see a mother puffin returning from the sea with six or eight sardines in her beak for feeding her young.

We come to the lighthouse and feel as if we are at the end of the earth as we view the sea from a lofty height, just as another horrendous storm approaches with more wind gusts and rain. A sodden walk back to the ferry marks another extraordinary day in the Faroes.

It's time to investigate the woollen knit shops that display the most exquisite knitwear, with their distinctive fair isle and ancient motifs. These garments are exported mainly to Denmark and are keenly sought. There is a store just adjacent to the town

square in Torshavn, and I enter to be greeted by a family of knitters, three generations working together.

It's hard to choose from the wonderful array of knitwear. The cost is eye watering but I realise that this is handiwork at its best, and buy a beautiful jacket that will last for years.

We settle into life in Torshavn over the next few days, walking the countryside trails and befriending the locals. Bleak, grey, rainy, desolate but fascinating, memories of the Faroes will remain with us always.

The Nile by Boat and Train

I have been a wanderer among distant fields,
I have sailed down mighty rivers

PERCY SHELLEY

We arrive in Cairo, having been told it is cheaper to organise a Nile Cruise by booking here than doing so at home. After adjusting to time changes and the chaos of Cairo, we find our way to a hole-in-the-wall business, and secure two berths on a Greek-owned ship leaving two days later.

To link with this departure we need to make a short flight to Luxor and so we board an ancient 707 aircraft that has seen better days and land in the surreal and wonderful world of ancient Egypt.

Nothing prepares you for the impact of this extraordinary place. We book into a small family-run hotel with a rooftop drinking space that overlooks the Nile in its regal splendour. In the distance lies the ancient city of Karnak and in the foreground the chaos of life with peddlers and touts doing their business among the stalls and boats on the Nile banks.

We spend the evening sitting at the rooftop bar, drinking reviving pomegranate tea and mingling with guests, who are mainly backpackers.

The ruins of Karnak are beckoning us the next day, and we set off at dawn when the light is muted and beautiful, to wander around the ruins of this ancient mix of religious monuments.

Karnak means fortified village. It comprises a vast mix of decayed temples, chapels and pylons, which form a series of processional gateways, linking the south by an avenue of sphinxes to the temple of Luxor, over three kilometres away. Its construction dates from 2000 BC, as part of the city of Thebes. Major construction took place when Thebes became the capital of ancient Egypt.

Every Pharaoh added something to this temple site constructing monuments, obelisks and pylons. In 323 AD Roman Emperor Constantine recognised the Christian religion and ordered the closing of pagan temples, so Karnak was abandoned and Christian churches were founded among the ruins.

It is eerily quiet and peaceful as we wander through the amazing structures, the early dawn light playing on the towering pylons and casting shadows along the way. We are hassled by touts, but we manage to fend them off and can discover the wonders of Karnak by ourselves. The plan is to join a guided tour at sunset, and so we return to the hotel, and after breakfast hire bikes.

By taking a ferry across the Nile we can ride to the Valley of the Queens, the burial site for the wives of the Pharaohs. Our bikes have seen better days but are fine and we go to the ferry stop to make the crossing to the western bank. No tourists are on the ferry and we join locals, families and commuters on a very overcrowded craft that heaves and groans across the water.

Disembarking, we set off riding slowly along stony pathways to the Valley of the Queens to view Nefertari's tomb, said to be the most beautiful in Egypt.

We park our bikes and wander into the tomb, and are

gobsmacked by its beauty, the colours and 3D design with hieroglyphic texts covering the walls and ceilings. King Rameses loved his wife and created the most beautiful tomb to honour her death. The scenes depict Nefertari being guided by the gods to her resting place.

Riding back we encounter a bus, jam packed with tourists. They are staring at us on our bikes in horror. We in turn love the fact that we're free from crowd herding and direction, and pedal on. Suddenly there's a puncture, and a severe one, that means we need to walk the remainder of the way to the ferry. It is hot and unforgiving, but we make it to the ferry and head back to the hotel.

By sunset we meet with our guide and other tourists to view Karnak at dusk and hear something of its history. Our guide is a professor from Cairo University, and he does not pause for breath. It is excruciating. I'm getting my Rameses and dynasties all mixed up, so I wander off by myself to meld with the extraordinary atmosphere, the shadows and the statues. As the moon rises over these amazing structures, I feel part of the ancient world of Egypt.

It is early morning and we are packed and ready for the Nile cruise, waiting to board as touts and traders pummel us with their wares. Finally on board and slowly departing we succumb to the pace of the Nile and recline on easy chairs to watch the world float by.

It is really an amazing sight, with tree palms at the river's edge; along the higher reaches camels saunter. The desert is dissected by this ancient river with fertile strips each side for cultivation but, further away, vast areas of stark, hot, arid sand.

Life on the boat is punctuated by meals. Mesmerised, we choose to stay on deck as the extraordinary world of the Nile reveals itself, reluctantly moving back to our cabin at night. After waking early, we once again take up our positions on deck.

Occasionally a narrow-bodied felucca will pass us. These traditional wooden sailing boats, with one or two canvas sails, are usually crewed by Nubians, indigenous to the region. The boats can take up to 10 people, and are still in active use as a means of transport on the Nile, and to ferry tourists from Luxor to Aswan.

We have befriended an Italian couple and spend an evening on deck playing 500, and with the Greek crew there are some hilarious misunderstandings with food and drink orders, not to mention rules of the game. This pattern of life continues for a week or so before we finally approach Aswan.

Nothing can prepare you for the impact of this place. There are feluccas everywhere. The river has widened and now has islands and inlets, tropical undergrowth, and huge flowering trees. Aswan straggles around its bank and is a hive of activity.

We check into a hotel and then return to the river to hire a rowing boat, a great way to explore the waters of this astounding place. Lord Kitchener's Island is our destination and we pull the oars and meander off, dodging feluccas and river craft, before finding a calm isolated area we are able to continue rowing in peace.

Lord Kitchener's Island was so named when he served as Consul-General to Egypt. It is oval shaped and sits plumb centre in the Nile at Aswan. Less then a kilometre in length it is now the site of the Aswan Botanical Gardens. Lord Kitchener had

transformed the island into a paradise of exotic trees and gardens, and a haven for rare and colourful birds.

We beach our boat in a small bay and wander through the trees, admiring the beds of colourful zinnias and the call of birds in the trees above us. It is cool and beautiful and silent after the turmoil and clutter of Aswan, and when we come to a cafe at the southern end of the island, we stop to take a reviving pomegranate tea, and immerse ourselves in the unbelievable tranquillity of the place.

We are due back in Cairo, and discover there are no daily flights, so we decide to catch a local bus to Luxor, and then get the overnight train to Cairo.

The bus station is hectic with milling passengers carrying so much luggage I would not be surprised to see a fridge or oven taken on board. We finally take our seats among this thronging humanity.

A few soldiers are scattered among the passengers, and I'm appalled to see a pregnant girl standing with others at the back, and no one offering her a seat. The young soldiers are well seated and discrimination of the worst kind comes to mind. I'm too far away to offer her a seat, but when the bus stops and she alights I press a cake of Chanel soap into her hand, and she turns to me with a glorious smile that transforms her face.

It is dusty, dirty, smelly and vile, but we finally make it to Luxor, and go to the train station to board the overnight train to Cairo. We've managed to book a sleeper, and just love the privacy after such a horrendous bus trip.

Egyptian rolling stock is probably 50 years old, and as we depart the clackety clack of the wheels is deafening, but the inside

of our compartment is clean, and we managed to buy supplies from the station shop to lessen the pangs of hunger. There are stops and starts, whistles and bells at each station, but we progress at such a frightening speed in between stops, that I'm amazed the train holds itself together.

Finally we pull into Cairo station, relieved and rested, marking the end of our Egyptian odyssey.

Kiev and Ukraine

A generation that ignores history has no past and no future

R.A. HEINLEIN

I am armed with a visa that has taken months to achieve through the Ukrainian Embassy in Canberra, where unfriendly and recalcitrant personnel kept delaying its progress. My bloke holds a British passport and does not need a visa. He is arriving the next day, so I'm all alone to face the barrage of officials at Immigration in Kiev.

There has been a computer glitch and I'm told to wait in the queue as each visa is hand processed. After two hours I finally enter a little office where one overworked and completely frazzled young man looks wearily at me, apologises, and then gets to work, marking every statement and stamping every page. Finally I'm free to go and walk through the gates to be met by a driver, who seems resigned to the wait time and is cheerful and welcoming.

The mighty Dnieper River winds its way through Kiev, the oldest capital in Europe, which existed as a commercial centre as early as the 5th century AD. It was a Slavic settlement on the trade route between Scandinavia and Constantinople. The Vikings took control in the 9th century, then the Mongols, then Poland, and finally Russia. Following the collapse of the Soviet Union, Ukraine declared independence in 1991.

Olena and Natalia walk the Artist's Street in Kiev.

Children present bouquets to the Chamber Group, Kiev, Ukraine.

The Dnieper is huge with parks and gardens lining its banks, as we wind along the boulevards to the Old Town. We reach the booked apartment, just off the square that is dominated by St Sophia's Cathedral, an enormous and beautiful landmark and a tribute to the Christian Orthodox religion in Ukraine.

The entrance to the apartment is bolted but one of the three keys I've been given gains entry to a marble foyer and lift. We go to the second floor and open the door to a spacious and lovely set of rooms with a family room overlooking the square.

History continues to unfold in Ukraine, as revolutions come and go. The current war with Russia on its eastern border is still smouldering. But there is a cultural rebellion underway, a creative wave sweeping the city. A long and winding street is devoted to artists, where paintings, drawing and sketching is done and often sold. There are handcraft streets displaying exquisite embroidery, where women are sewing and knitting, and dotted between are vintage cafes with people milling together, meeting for coffee and patronising the handmade goods on offer.

It's a total surprise to experience the hum and buzz of a city determined to shake off the shadow of Russia and retain and rebuild its culture, and glory in its unique history.

I decide a hair appointment might be fun as I wander the streets of the Old Town, and come to a very upmarket-looking salon. I am greeted by a flamboyant and effusive owner, sporting a fringe with closely clipped sides, a silk scarf wound casually around his neck, and wearing a silk smock. He speaks some English and ushers me into the washroom where I sink into a leather chair with the massagers going, listening to gentle classical music as he washes my hair.

Then its off to the main arena, where he cuts and blow dries with practised expertise, talking and laughing as he does so. The whole experience is a joy and delight, and I emerge ready to sight see.

Parks and gardens line the Dnieper River, alive with people meeting, picnicking, busking, dancing – all enjoying the glorious weather and the great outdoors. Most people live in small apartments, and so the parks are the way they can commune with nature and enjoy community life. There are pop-up cafes and ice cream stalls dotted around, seats and enclaves where you can sit in peace and view the exquisite gardens, fountains and arbors.

I wind my way back to the city and find Maidan, the square in the centre of the city. This is the traditional place for political rallies, and also a regular site for non-political events like Christmas fairs and New Year celebrations. An underground shopping mall was built beneath the square to replace the old underpass, and this has become a mecca for locals and tourists alike.

Climbing the steep pavements back to the Old Town, I wander over to Saint Sophia's Cathedral, crossing paths with a monk in a flowing purple gown. He nods to me and then speaks English, asking me if I would like to see inside. I follow him into what is Kiev's oldest standing church, its mosaics and frescoes date back to 1017 AD.

Centuries of history engulf this church. The frescoes are wonderful and the icons and paintings beautifully displayed, often with altars in front of a particular saint. There are candles to be lit, and people quietly praying and moving from icon to

icon. Scarves are worn and there is an atmosphere of peace and tranquillity, occasionally disturbed by the tolling of a bell.

My monk bids me farewell and I go to the bell tower, which has a mammoth staircase, but well worth the climb to get a bird's-eye view of the cathedral complex and a panoramic view of Kiev. Then I wander back to the apartment and prepare for my bloke's arrival and the christening we've come to Ukraine to attend.

We assemble at the Church of St Michael, scarved and gowned, with the little one resplendent in a traditional christening dress. The Priest sports a ponytail and has a gorgeous sense of humour.

We go into a small chapel surrounded by icons and frescoes with a huge baptismal font in the centre. The service is in Ukrainian, and we watch in fascination as he blesses the child, the parents and godparents, and then immerses the baby's head into the water for the final blessing. A scream of surprise is the response, but soon quelled, and we all troop outside into the glorious sunshine for photos, and make our way to a nearby restaurant to celebrate.

After a few days of family outings we decide to take a train to Liviv, the largest city in West Ukraine, and one of its main cultural centres. Initially it belonged to the Habsburgs, but after the Soviet invasion of 1939, it became part of the Soviet Union. In 1991, after the collapse of the Soviet Union, independence was achieved, and Liviv became part of Ukraine.

This UNESCO-listed city exudes authentic central European charm, rather like Prague and Krakow did before tourism engulfed them. Liviv did not succumb to Soviet degradation, and its coffee houses, rattling trams and cobbled streets show you that the candle of Ukrainian national identity is staying well lit.

The Opera House, theatres, ballet and art continue to thrive and prosper from their ancient beginnings with writers, artists, and poets thronging together in their enclaves. The entire city seems to be focused on the arts.

After an exhausting morning of walking the streets, we stop for a coffee at a little vintage cafe that spills onto the pavement. Suddenly there is screaming and a rumpus as two gypsies, one very pregnant, run for their lives along the cobbled street. They have been caught stealing, and the owner of the shop is in hot pursuit, but they are too quick for him and disappear along a laneway.

We settle back and watch buskers in competition, one playing a violin, and the other a piano, and further along the roadway a girl has her ghetto blaster playing pop music, and she is dancing, with a turned-up cap for people to drop their coins in.

In the centre of town a stage is being set up for an outdoor concert, and people are placing chairs and tables around the stage. An antique tram rattles along the road. It has one carriage and does a ring route of the city all day, free of charge.

We are enchanted by Liviv. It has retained its culture and character throughout wars and turbulence, and remained virtually untouched. We reluctantly take the intercity train back to Kiev, and then wend our way home.

Swimming with Whale Sharks

Freedom is the last and best hope of earth

ABRAHAM LINCOLN

The mysterious and elusive whale shark prefers the warm water of the tropics, populating all the tropical seas of the planet. Many migrate every spring to the continental shelf off Western Australia, where the coral spawning on the Ningaloo Reef provides an abundant supply of plankton. They will patiently wait for as long as 14 hours for fish to spawn on the reef before, like a slow-moving filter, they glide in to eat the eggs, mouth wide open as they feed close to the water's surface.

Their unique pattern of spots is like the human fingerprint, marking every shark as an individual. They have a flattened head and blunt snout, dorsal fins and a huge dual-lobed tail fin and although up to 12 metres in length they are docile, allowing swimmers to approach as they glide along.

The female whale shark produces eggs, but the young hatch inside the mother instead of the water. She then gives birth to about 300 live young, but most don't make it to maturity. They have a long childhood, producing their own offspring when 25 years of age, and potentially living for a century.

We gather at the wharf in Exmouth to board a small launch and take off for Ningaloo Reef. John, our guide, is a character with dreadlocks, an athletic physique and twinkling eyes. He instructs us to clamber into wetsuits, and I manage to do so

back to front, so need to repeat the process before I'm zipped up and ready to go. But we won't need diving equipment with the sharks swimming close to the surface.

We take goggles with a breathing tube and scan the water. When we see bubbles coming to the surface in the distance, John instructs the driver to go closer and then to cut the engine.

We tentatively immerse, noticing the warmth of the water. John has taken the lead and is swimming ahead, so we follow him. Suddenly he stops and says, 'Dive down a little, there are two huge manta rays approaching us.'

Described as the gentle giants of the sea, I see two rays following each other, gliding and waving their diamond-shaped bodies as they move forward. These highly intelligent creatures are probably curious as to our presence in their territory.

Manta means blanket or cover in Spanish, which explains their appearance. I take a deep breath and dive down to get closer to them. They hover around me and I swim slowly around them before having to return to the surface to breathe. When I return to the depths I see they are moving on, gently waving their huge wingspans to propel themselves, mouths open, gathering plankton and krill.

We continue to swim toward the bubbles and John stops swimming and alerts us to the whale sharks, directly below us. I take a deep breath and dive, and there it is, a huge animal with the typical white spots in concentric patterns all over its body resting just below the surface of the water. I swim closer and touch its body; it feels like silk.

We all swim with this whale shark, marvelling at the gentle temperament and lazy attitude of this mammoth creature, free

of predators. It has the freedom to roam through its ocean playground, spending the days lolling in peace and solitude.

We spend an hour swimming with him, exploring his length and the enormous tail fin. He is not perturbed by our presence, gently drifting along, his mouth open to gather krill as he goes.

To swim with two giants of the deep and briefly enter their world, so far removed from ours, has been a life-changing experience. We decide to support marine life conservation on our return to Exmouth.

The Czech Republic

(1998)

I am the inferior of any man whose rights I trample underfoot

HORACE GREENLEY

In November 1989 student protesters filled the streets of Prague, eight days after the collapse of the Berlin Wall. They were soon joined by citizens of all ages in their thousands, taking over Wenceslas Square and finally forcing out the Communist regime. This peaceful transition of power became known as the Velvet Revolution.

It is 1998, and we are off to see the new Czech Republic, having been invited to stay with friends of friends, who live about 45 minutes from the centre of Prague. We are greeted by Svata and Ivana and shown into their spacious and lovely apartment. We settle in to chat with them about the mammoth changes in their country. Life was tough, grim and boring during the Communist regime, with your every move monitored and recorded, but Svata has a small *dacha* in the countryside where they could escape to, and he would fish and Ivana relax away from the humdrum and boredom of Prague.

Svata is an architect and worked through the regime designing buildings for the government. It was slow and arduous but they survived reasonably well. They have no children. Now their world has changed, with wonderful food flooding in from all over Europe and the shops filled with the latest goods. Wenceslas Square is the bustling centre of commerce and the heart and soul of Prague.

We decide to go there and walk to the nearest train station. Our carriage is crowded with people; the young looking cool and fashion conscious. They are animated, chatting excitedly to each other, whereas the old seem to wear a mantle left over from the former regime, cowed and uncertain, fearful of the changes in their lives. There are no rigid rules to obey, no queues to dictate who shops first. In this free market everything is available, and there is a frenetic rush by the young to adopt this new way of life as quickly as possible.

But the aged, treated like rats on a treadmill for years, are confused and disorientated when the treadmill was suddenly removed.

On arrival we walk to the square. It is huge, surrounded by buildings from a different age, but with the occasional Soviet-style construction between the gorgeous architecture. The place is buzzing with open stalls and pop-ups, buskers and touts. We are constantly asked to change currency, with the current problem being galloping inflation. We soon discover that there are two rates, one for tourists and one for locals, and hard currency from any other country is preferable to the Czech Koruna.

We walk to the Old Town, or Stare Mesto, a cobblestoned hub with the astronomical clock standing plumb centre. This was a medieval settlement, separated from the outside by a semi-circular moat. The Charles Bridge crosses the Vltava river leading to the lesser town of Prague, known as the Malá Strana.

The Old Town features a bustling market square and the historic Jewish Quarter. We watch the clock chime and four figures flanking the clock are set in motion, with a window above the clock opening to the mechanical walking of the Apostles.

After this performance a trumpet player heralds the beginning of the next hour. It is mesmerising, taking us back to a medieval era when time was measured slowly and deliberately. We decide to take a coffee and just while away an hour in order to watch the performance once more.

The square is surrounded by pastel-coloured buildings and dominated by the Church of Our Lady before Týn, with its Gothic twin spires and pointed arches. Classical concerts are conducted here and we decide to attend one later in the day.

One of the main attractions in Prague is to walk across the Charles Bridge that lies adjacent to the town square. Built in 1357 AD, it is flanked by two Gothic bridge towers and lined with magnificent baroque statues of religious figures. At every turn in Prague, there is something astounding and aesthetically magnificent to admire and think about.

We decide to investigate Josefov, the Jewish Quarter, a small area between the Old Town square and the Vltava river. There is a square surrounded by houses where Jews had lived for centuries. Academics and scholars, musicians and artists worked in Prague, but they lived here together. During the Second World War they were rounded up by the Nazis and shot; 90% of the Jewish population was eradicated.

I sense the horror. It seems to me that the buildings in this enclave speak for all the dead souls, and there is a sense that this atrocity still lives in the square. The Prague Symphony Orchestra was largely Jewish and it disappeared, the university was devoid of academics. Repercussions from this ethnic elimination continued for decades. We go to a nearby bar and order something strong to try to blot out what we have just seen in Josefov.

Soon its time for the evening concert in the Church of Our Lady before Týn, and mercifully it will be Mozart, positive and happy. It is two dollars a ticket and the church is packed with locals and a few tourists. The glorious music engulfs the church and we emerge feeling more at peace with the world.

Our final destination is the Tatra Mountains. To break our journey we take the train to Olomouc in the province of Moravia. In a way Olomouc is Moravia's version of Prague with its architecture, religious heritage and culture emanating from Roman times preserved. Subsequently it became a Habsburg stronghold, and this university town, practically unknown outside the Czech Republic, has survived wars and turbulence intact.

An imposing cathedral, monasteries, an astronomical clock, castles and an ancient opera house on the town square are just some of the delights to explore, and we end the day by attending an opera by Offenbach, having bought two box seats for two dollars. The theatre is packed with locals of all ages and the performance is astounding, reinforcing my understanding that the arts thrived and was protected and encouraged during the communist era.

Our magical day in Olomouc ends with our walk back to our little hotel, across cobblestones with the moonlight casting a pale light on the towers and spires.

Taking a train to Starý Smokovec is a three-hour traverse of rural villages and verdant countryside. We are heading for the High Tatras, a mountain range that divides Slovakia with Poland. It is the smallest high-altitude range of mountains in the world, and is protected as a UNESCO biosphere reserve.

Being quite remote, the Tatras have chamois, brown bears, wolves and wild boar roaming around, but we think they are probably hibernating in this clear and freezing winter weather.

Armed with rather old ski equipment, we head to the little ski resort by funicular, and find a single, slow, very cold chairlift. The piste is ungroomed and dangerous, so the day of skiing ends early as we huddle around the fire back at our little hostel in Starý Smokovec. The architecture is interesting in this town with the occasional building turreted, spired and shrouded by forest, inspiring stories of Dracula and vampires.

We decide hiking is a better alternative to skiing. It is Sunday and a clear, cold and sunny day. We pass a tiny church that is conducting a service and wander inside to sit at the back and watch proceedings. The parishioners have filled the pews in this Lutheran church. The minister acknowledges our presence and we follow the procedure not understanding a word, but enjoying being part of the service. Religion was forbidden during the Communist regime, and now people of all ages have flocked back to church.

As I write this 20 years on, I acknowledge the transformation of the Czech Republic has been astounding. It is now a powerhouse in Western Europe.

African Safari, Namibia

There is no fear without some hope,
and no hope without some fear

BARUCH SPINOZA

Three-hours driving from Windhoek, Namibia, takes us to the Old Traders Lodge within the Erindi Private Game Reserve. It is sited on a dam with rondavels facing a waterhole, and immediately we are transported to the wilds of Africa.

There are three elephants gently bathing and luxuriating in the water. One fills his trunk and sloshes water all over his back, while the others drink and flap their ears. They know we are watching them, and yet totally ignore us.

There are a number of wildebeest nearby in a small group, taking water before moving on. Warthogs are trotting close to the water's edge, with guinea fowl foraging close by.

In this paradise, you do not need to travel to see game. Just being at the waterhole brings every species of animal to your attention, and to my surprise it seems that every species has its turn. Giraffe are waiting in line and will replace the elephants. A rhino wanders by. Impala and waterbuck await their turn to approach the water.

The restaurant is open to the weather. It overlooks the dam where crocodile loll around at the far end, sunning themselves. Closer to the restaurant there are elephants sauntering and

hippos, nocturnal grazers, are immersed in the water, waiting for dusk. A hippo opens his huge mouth baring two long teeth. He yawns and grunts distinctively before dipping back into the water with his eyes just above the surface, surveying it all.

Suddenly we see a chase. A team of 18 wild dogs are chasing a kudu. She takes refuge in the water, just far enough away from her predators. The dogs seem to know what they are doing and immediately circle the dam, three on the restaurant side, the others circle around. The long wait begins. The kudu will not move from the safety of the water for hours, waiting until the dogs tire of the pursuit and move on to another victim.

Nighttime brings all the sounds of the bush with shadows and outlines of animals either taking water, or retreating to the safety of bushland. The nocturnal predators are emerging. We see a female lion on the hunt for food. She probably has cubs nearby and is the prime hunter as the male of the pride is bone lazy. He waits for the prey to be delivered to him; his main role is to keep an eye on the pride.

We leave Erindi bound for a private reserve run by a female colleague, through the global mission for rhino conservation. This very large estate, bordered by mountains, was established by one of southern Africa's most prominent conservationists. There are guards and electrified fences and closed-circuit cameras to protect the rhinos in her care.

From time to time orphaned babies are brought here to be nurtured. They have been traumatised by seeing their mothers killed and mutilated for rhino horn, and are often found whimpering at their mother's side. A slow and gentle rehabilitation takes place. The baby is never left alone, being

Heather with Tilda and Emmy in Namibia.

Tilda with an orphan baby rhino,
Namibia, 2018.

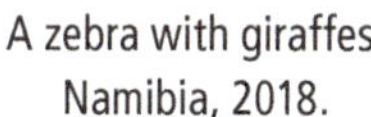

A zebra with giraffes,
Namibia, 2018.

hand fed milk and gradually adjusting to this new life. It is time consuming and labour intensive, but very successful.

The Namibian Government is working hand-in-hand with this reserve, trying to counter the shocking demand for rhino horn and the people who will risk everything to poach these gentle creatures. There are signs of success here, unlike South Africa, where rhino poaching has become an epidemic.

We enter the security fortress and drive along a winding road, bordered by a river. An elephant on the road blocks our way. He has all the time in the world as he grazes on a huge branch he has felled, eyeing us off as he proceeds, seeming to enjoy the fact he is preventing us from moving. Finally with a snort and a flapping of his ears, he removes the branch to the side of the road, and allows us to pass.

Inge is there to meet us and we go to her private residence shrouded by trees and overlooking a distant mountain range. We sit on an open terrace with warthogs trotting around and buck gently passing by.

The Namibian Government has declared zero tolerance for rhino poaching and the instances are dropping, but Inge took possession of a little one two weeks ago. The baby is thriving and would we like to see him?

We climb into her jeep and make our way to an enclosure, where a carer is waiting for us. There he is, small vulnerable and eagerly drinking his milk from a specially designed bottle. He demands four-hourly feeds, and someone is with him 24/7. Inge takes a turn in tending him and has become his mother figure. He nuzzles up to her and stands meekly by her side. There is a covered area for him to sleep and that's just about all he does,

sleeping and drinking the milk. When he is about 18 months old he will be introduced to the herd.

Inge has about 80 rhinos on her property, heavily guarded and secreted away. No one knows exactly how many she has or where they have their habitat. The reserve is large and can easily shield them from outside attention. We visit the area and see rhinos everywhere, in family groups, solitary males, happily living their lives in the wild away from human interference and its tragic outcomes.

The Namibian Government has divided the country into conservatories, and the local people are proudly part of this initiative. They are employed to protect, preserve and nurture each area and proudly compete with each other as to which conservatory is best. Through this initiative the local people are far less likely to destroy habitats, or become involved with poaching. There are money-making enterprises associated, with the tourist dollar making its way to the African community through handcrafts and gift shops around the reserves.

Namibia is a fine example of what can be achieved to encourage a balance between wildlife and human life with both sides benefiting and prospering.

Saint Petersburg

(2012)

A smooth sea never made a skilled mariner

ENGLISH PROVERB

Living in Sweden and being so close to Saint Petersburg is the catalyst to visit. I decide to take along my daughter-in-law to see the sights, attend ballet and opera and to immerse ourselves in Russian culture.

A Swedish passport gains easy entry for Kerstin but my visa involves months of filling out forms and answering questions that seem more like something you would do if working for Intelligence. Finally I'm granted a visa and we set of to Gothenburg to fly to Saint Petersburg.

The airport is rather grim and we join a long queue for Immigration before heading to a small hotel in the centre of Saint Petersburg. It is late autumn with a chill in the air, so we decide on a Russian meal in the hotel restaurant and I'm astounded to see the bar dotted with locals who are dressed in flamboyant clothes, mini skirts and fish-net stockings are everywhere, but with the trusty overcoat lying close by.

We sit at the bar for a drink and manage a stilted conversation with a girl, who suggests we start with borscht soup followed by piroshki, small dumplings filled with cabbage, mushrooms or meat. The borscht is just delicious, almost pureed beetroot as a

hot soup, and the piroshki is also a perfect prelude to wandering the streets of Saint Petersburg to take in the sights.

Nevsky Prospect, established in 1703 with the founding of the city, is the main boulevard. Between the shops and commercial outlets there is the Stroganoff Palace, The Kazan Cathedral, the Art Nouveau Book House, an 18th-century shopping mall, and the Anichkov Bridge resplendent with horse statues.

We walk to the 18th-century shopping mall and pass babushkas sweeping the streets, glamorous young things window shopping, families out walking – all among the hum and buzz of traffic. This centuries-old shopping mall is large and houses antique train shops, a stamp collectors outlet, book stalls with antique books, and music and instrument shops with sheet music for sale. I sense that people here revere what is old, love their arts and music, worship their literary giants and feed off a culture that has survived constant regime change and turbulence.

Someone is reading Tolstoy to a large crowd of people of all ages in front of the library. It is a cold bleak weekend, yet families gather to hear the works of one of their greatest authors. Inside the library, Pushkin is being read to a group of avid listeners. Everywhere we walk, there are crowds taking in the joys of the Russian culture.

We come to a park and see a pop-up stall and buy hot chocolates to fend off the cold. There is a fountain and curved seats nearby to sit and just take in the atmosphere. Being late autumn there are no tourists and it's fun to blend in with the locals.

We rest back at the hotel before putting on our glad rags to attend the opera *La Boheme* at the Mariinsky Theatre. This magnificent theatre was built in 1860; it was here the masters of

Russian culture staged their premieres. Tchaikovsky, Mussorgsky and Rimsky-Korsakov, to name just a few.

The mezzanine is full before the performance and we order champagne and watch the patrons milling around and congregating. It is wonderful to have dressed for opera and to see the locals of Saint Petersburg have done the same in their velvets and furs, children with their hair tied back with satin ribbons, and a sprinkling of dinner suits.

It is time to take our seats, and the drama and beauty of the theatre is revealed, its balconies and boxes, and a huge chandelier dangling from the central dome. Needless to say the performance is astounding and we walk back to the hotel in a heady state. Most of the patrons seem to be walking as well, in stockings and flimsy high-heeled shoes but with heavy coats over their evening clothes to combat the chilly conditions.

Waking late, we decide to visit the Literary Cafe for breakfast before moving on to the Hermitage. Situated on Nevsky Prospect, this cafe was frequented by famous writers of Russian literature, including Pushkin and Dostoyevsky. It started as a confectionary shop, and in 1837 Pushkin went there before attending his fatal duel. It morphed into a restaurant and Tchaikovsky is said to have been there when he ordered a glass of water infected with cholera, causing his death.

Such drama and tragedy is part of Russian life, and we enter to drink not coffee but Russian tea, served from a samovar. It is cozy and welcoming, and we hear that poetry readings are held here from time to time. There is a waxwork of Pushkin, and pictures of Russian writers hang on the walls. We drag ourselves into the outside chill to walk to the Hermitage Museum.

The Hermitage was founded in 1764 when the Empress, Catherine the Great, acquired an impressive collection of paintings from Berlin. She then commanded her ambassadors around the world to purchase the best art they could find.

We realise the impossibility of seeing it all and so choose the Dutch Golden Age, displayed along the southern facade of the gallery. These wonderful paintings by van Dyck, Rubens, Rembrandt and many others encapsulate an era of art that emanated from Holland, and today there are strong connections with Amsterdam to allow exchanges of the paintings so Holland can claim some ownership of their artistic heritage.

The Hermitage sits in the grounds of the Winter Palace, the official residence of the Russian emperors from 1732 until the Russian Revolution in 1917. We walk through the magnificence of the Palace, the architraves and ornate ceilings seemingly stretching forever. You could spend a week investigating the Hermitage and still not see it all.

On our final night we see *The Vampire's Ball*, a modern musical set in Transylvania, and staged at the Saint Petersburg Comedy Theatre. This hit show is totally booked out and once again the patrons dress up for their evening out. Ghouls and vampires prowl the audience and the young and innocent female sings exquisitely from the stage. It is stunning and wonderful, and again we emerge in a lightheaded state to walk our way back to the hotel.

We have been totally seduced by Saint Petersburg and all it has to offer, and are reluctant to leave it behind as we head home to Sweden.

Fort Portal, Uganda

As long as our civilisation is essentially one of property,
of fences,
it will be mocked by delusions

RALPH WALDO EMERSON

We are in Kampala, Uganda, and are planning a road trip to Fort Portal, in the south-west of the country, from where we shall branch off to see the chimps, a wetland, and a bird sanctuary. We have our driver, Goodluck, and a reasonable old car so we decide to take the rural road to Fort Portal instead of the bituminised highway on the other side of the river. Unfortunately it is too late to turn back when we realise the rural road has never been maintained and is littered with potholes and ridge traps. The going is slow with many crossings of riverbeds and a hilly bushy terrain.

Goodluck smokes foul-smelling cigarettes, but is hugely entertaining and funny so we wind the windows down and let him smoke away. We come to a large river crossing and see local youths using it as a car wash, receiving money for sloshing cars with the river water, talking and laughing and having a ball as they work on a queue of cars. We cross the river and prepare to endure another four hours of agony before we arrive at Fort Portal. where we check into a local hotel and order strong gin and tonics to while away the sunset.

We are up early for our day in the forest, driving around the most beautiful field of crater lakes. Steep sided and pristine they

border the lush tropical rain forest of Kibale. This ancient forest is home to monkeys, baboons and even forest elephants. The chimpanzees were successfully habituated here in 1986.

Goodluck takes us deeper into the forest and we see monkeys and baboons but no chimps. It is shaded, lush and beautiful as we walk here, taking in the presence of nature untouched by humans.

Suddenly a rustle of leaves above us reveals a chimp swinging from a tree branch before gently alighting on the next tree. We wait to see if he is accompanied by a troop, and sure enough they are following him.

Chimps rarely sit still during the day, they are constantly active, sorting out their status within the group, pursuing a female, tending to their young or just playing about in the forest. They completely ignore us as they continue their journey. This glimpse of the troop is all we shall see of them, but it's wonderful to experience chimps in the wild, healthy and free.

Next day we once again rise early, this time to explore the Bigodi Wetland Sanctuary. I'm unprepared for the hundreds of subsistence holdings of local Africans. The population explosion has certainly occurred here and we survey a countryside taken over by smallholdings and villages. The wetland itself has been reduced by these holdings to a slither of land strongly bordered by fences and housing. It is a huge disappointment as we enter, with the momentary peace eroded by all the activity outside. A pathway of sunken logs leads to the most beautiful environment of ferns, trees and flowers, butterflies, bees and birds. This pristine pocket of exquisite nature has been severely reduced by the burgeoning population.

We are now heading to Ndali Lodge with our trusty Goodluck at the wheel negotiating a track over a ridge that leads to the lodge, perched on the edge of a crater lake. We are at the foot of the Rwenzori Mountains, where the great Rift Valley meets the Congo Basin. There is a main thatched cottage for the restaurant meals and cottages for 16 guests that face the west to view the Mountains of the Moon. With no electricity it is candlelight dinners and a candle for bedtime. The mountain tracks that lead to the cottages are open passways used by bats, owls and frogs to gain access to the crater lake.

It is hard to describe the beauty of this place, built on a ridge that leads down to the water. There are flowering shrubs everywhere and a narrow terrace where you can take breakfast and watch the butterflies and bees. The amazing variety of birds fills the air with birdsong. I think this place must be close to paradise.

A large kiln-like structure is in fact the furnace to heat water and Jimbo is stoking the fire constantly to allow us to have hot showers. We subside into the most tranquil existence, birdwatching, reading and walking before the drama of a dinner by candlelight.

We return to the cottage with its small balcony to watch the mystic drama of the Mountains of the Moon. By sheer luck a full moon is casting its light on these extraordinary peaks, and lingers there in a glorious boast of prominence. It is easy to understand how legends and stories have emanated from this sight; it dwarfs us humans, we insignificant observers to this panoramic world.

The next drive is to visit a tea plantation, and again we see the encroachment of the natural environment to acres and acres

of carefully tended tea plants. The government is corrupt, and those who fight to keep areas pristine have little hope with the tea industry's expansion into former untouched areas. So, although beautiful and lush, it is with disappointment that we view this hive of industry.

We decide to take the bituminised road back to Kampala, and although sealed, it is narrow and takes every truck from the west to Kampala. This trip too is slow and arduous, but at least smooth and we drive to the centre of the city.

There are storks nesting in the main street in a medium-sized tree, oblivious to the activity around them. The mother spreads her wings and then sits on the nest, with the father watching close by. This is the image that stays with me in beautiful over-populated Uganda.

Fish River Canyon, Namibia

Nature goes on her way,
and all that seems an exception is really
according to order

JOHANN VON GOETHE

A decision to see the Fish River Canyon means designing a tour to the southern region of Namibia, so we secure the services of a driver and car in Windhoek. There are huge distances to cover so we leave early with Happy Harry at the wheel. A local Namibian, Harry loves his moniker and welcomes us to his car and the long drive ahead. Fortunately he does not smoke, and likes silence between his bursts of guiding, so it is a very pleasant trip.

We reach the outskirts of Windhoek, Namibia's capital, and are at once in a world of arid isolation, with the narrow road carving through the desolate landscape. But not for long as grasses, shrubs and trees denote a change of climate; fields of lupins grow each side of the road. A wandering ostrich is stalking the terrain and close by some antelopes. We stop at a roadside table with a gazebo roof and take a pause for drinks and contemplation of this landscape.

Namibia is one of the least populated countries in Africa and this lack of human habitation seems to emphasise its vastness. Finally we arrive at Ai-Ais, and the Canyon. It is late and we check into our hotel for an early night. Ai-Ais means 'burning

water' referring to the sulphurous hot springs that lie under the riverbed of the Fish River forming an oasis for the extremely arid landscape. The water, with an average temperature of 60°C, is pumped into a series of indoor pools at the resort. Our room adjoins one of these indoor pools and we promise ourselves a dip after exploring the Canyon.

The Fish River Canyon, the second largest in the world (after the Grand Canyon), was formed 120 million years ago when the Gondwana continent separated from the African continent. This allowed the river to erode further into the rock, forming a canyon 549 metres deep. It is Namibia's greatest geological wonder, extending for 161 kilometres and ending at Ai-Ais with the Hell's Corner riverbend.

Happy Harry is up for the trek so we all walk along a narrow track heading for the Canyon, through landscape rocky and desolate. Suddenly we are at a precipice overlooking a vast open space of enormous proportions. There are birds flying below us and a swirl of mist that gathered overnight is slowly lifting, revealing creases and rocky outcrops. Far below the Fish River is winding its way between the rocks.

Harry leads us down one of the tracks and it feels as if we are entering an entirely new world, one that you could bypass if you were unaware of the Canyon's source. We get to the Fish River and gaze up at the cliff face with its extraordinary structure, contemplating history going back millions of years.

The temperature is rising with midday approaching so it's a hot and sweaty climb back to the top, and a rush to the hotel to cool off. It's time to test the sulphuric waters at the resort, which are pleasantly warm and caressing but the ever-present smell of

sulphur is rather overpowering. People with arthritic conditions and skeletal pain come here to take the waters, with significant success. For us it is a reviving and wonderful way to ease back from our Canyon adventure.

We are now heading for Swakopmund (German for mouth of the Swakop) situated on the southern coast. It is now a beach resort but was founded as a German settlement in 1892. Although a coastal town, it is in the middle of the Namibian desert, with shifting sand dunes that tower above and eventually retreat to the sea. The water table beneath the desert seeps its way to the coast, forming an extraordinary wetland wedged between the desert and the sea, its freshwater vegetation sustained by the underground aquifer.

The best way to explore these wonders is by quad bike, and we meet up with Mike, our quad bike guide, to scale the dunes and head toward the wetland. Mike revs up his bike and we follow suit, with the three of us taking off at a nice steady pace before we hit the dunes. They are very high and quite forbidding, but the bikes are stable and the tyres stay on the surface of the sand to allow us to climb.

From the top of the dunes we see the Atlantic Ocean, vast and forbidding along the Skeleton Coast. This coastline is so named because of all the shipwrecks over the centuries. The waters on this side of Africa are treacherous and have claimed many lives.

We park the bikes and walk to the wetland, a sliver of fertility between the dunes and the sea. There are ferns and shrubs, with birds, and bees buzzing around. We can see the pristine freshwater seeping from beneath the sand dunes into this extraordinary space.

Back on our bikes we head off on the homeward journey. On descending a dune, my bloke manages to tip his bike over. He scrambles free with his bike upturned, wheels in the air. Mike tells us that in all his years of quad bike guiding, he has never seen such a performance. He turns the bike back on its wheels and a contrite husband remounts, vowing to never again twist the steering wheel sharply on a downward slope.

We take a break on another dune's peak for wine and cheese and time to appreciate the wonders of western Namibia, before heading back to Swakopmund. Happy Harry greets us and we tell him of our adventures on the dunes as we drive back to Windhoek.

Monarto Safari Park, South Australia

The more an idea is developed,
the more concise becomes its expression

ALFRED BOUGEART

Monarto was a proposed satellite city for Adelaide, and when this was overruled, the land was given to Adelaide Zoo for a peppercorn rent. Closed to the public, it was a breeding facility for endangered species and an adjustment area for animals from the zoo.

This was 1983 and by 1993 it had developed into an open-range zoo, with bus and walking tours for the public. Covering 1600 hectares the scope for its development was just beginning.

It is 2020 and Monarto Zoological Park has become Monarto Safari Park. There are plans for a five-star luxury Wild Africa accommodation facility to complement the attractions of visiting a park that has animals living as close to their original habitats as possible with boundless space.

On entering the gates a group of emus can be seen slowly stalking the roadside. This would be the father with his chicks. The mother simply lays the eggs and, abandoning responsibility, wanders off into the bush. The father sits on the nest and hatches the chicks.

We follow the long and winding road through dense bushland to the Visitor Centre, a sleepy lizard slowly crossing the road in front of us. A group of white-winged choughs can be seen bickering. Black, but with white tips on their wings, they are community focused, and communally build a huge mud nest, hatch and nurture the chicks and forage together.

We decide to use the walking trails to see the Park and head toward the rock wallaby enclosure, its rocky outcrops mirroring the natural habitat of these small and beautiful marsupials. There are wallabies peering at us from the highest rocks as we wander along the central path. Their unusual colouring and copper-coloured striped tails were the reason for their demise in colonial days, when they were hunted almost to extinction. Breeding and resettlement in the southern Flinders Ranges has been a very successful enterprise, and we view some of the animals that form part of this program.

Walking across a dry creek bed, we come to the chimpanzee enclosure, opened by Dr Jane Goodall who maintained it was the best enclosure of its kind in the world. It is huge, with a night quarters and a sloped outdoor area with waterfalls and trees connected by ropes, so we see the chimps climbing, tumbling and playing together.

One old chimp sits on an overhead platform with a blanket over his head, deep in thought. There are 14 chimps of varying ages and stages in the troop, and we are mesmerised watching them all.

A winding steep path leads to the Ridge Track, which will connect us to the Waterhole Function Centre and the giraffe

platform. We walk along the path, noticing callitris trees, an Australian native pine that can live for up to 300 years. Often covered in lichen, it is an indicator of the pristine environment at Monarto. Circular diggings indicate that echidnas have been busy here, and blue wrens and honeyeaters fly from tree to tree. Suddenly we hear the raucous call of a Mallee ringneck parrot, as two off them swoop low over us, the luminous yellow feathers around their necks making them instantly recognizable.

Arriving at the waterhole, we walk along the giraffe platform to watch a keeper feed the giraffes. The platform is high enough that you are eye-to-eye with the giraffe. You can see his beautiful long eyelashes and 17-centimetre tongue, which he now wraps around the browse he's offered.

Monarto has produced 48 giraffes over the years, some of which have been transferred to other zoos around Australia. There are around 20 giraffes in the enclosure today, some are coming over to take browse, some are drinking from the waterhole, others are gently walking to a shady spot. Eland and zebra share this huge enclosure. It shares a climate and vegetation with southern Africa, so they feel totally at home.

We walk back to the waterhole and over a bridge to a steep and winding track that leads us to the rhino bomas. There are seven white rhinos here, gathered together with the latest baby, gently grazing and wallowing in the mud pool. They see us and wander over to be patted, and as they are humanised, they are happy and eager to be close to us.

Monarto's rhino program began in 2002 and has steadily expanded and progressed. It is now the premier rhino facility in the South East Asian region.

A program to bring rhinos from South Africa has begun, to establish a large insurance population to counter the shocking statistics of rhino poaching in Africa.

We now take the Carnivore Track, which winds across another section of the Park to the Windara Platform, where we can view the lions. There are 12 lions in the pride, and with four new cubs it is an entertaining visit. The cubs are playing around the females, climbing and rolling, biting their tails, as the mother and aunties looking on with forbearance. The males are a short distance away ignoring them totally.

There are still wild dogs, hyenas, and Tassie devils to visit, and a cheetah platform, built to view the precious pack of Cheetah, who are thriving and breeding here at Monarto.

So in 25 years, what began as a token adjustment facility has become a world-renowned open-range reserve, saving endangered species from extinction.

Printed in Australia
AUHW012050010321
341907AU00001B/1

9 781743 058091